FRANCIS FRITH'S
TOWN & CITY
MEMORIES

BUXTON

A life-long Buxtonian, COLIN WELLS is known to many
in the town, not only as a local historian and author but as a
radiographer who has worked at Buxton Hospital since 1972.

HALL GARDENS C1865 2795

FRANCIS FRITH'S

TOWN & CITY

MEMORIES

BUXTON

COLIN WELLS

FRANCIS FRITH'S

TOWN&CITY
MEMORIES

First published as Buxton, A Photographic History of your Town
in 2001 by Black Horse Books, an imprint of The Francis Frith Collection
Revised edition published in the United Kingdom in 2006 by
The Francis Frith Collection as Buxton, Town and City Memories
Limited Hardback Edition ISBN 1-84589-118-X
Paperback Edition ISBN 1-84589-119-8

British Library Cataloguing in Publication Data

Buxton
Town and City Memories
Colin Wells

The Francis Frith Collection®
Frith's Barn, Teffont,
Salisbury, Wiltshire SP3 5QP
Tel: +44 (0) 1722 716 376
Email: info@francisfrith.co.uk
www.francisfrith.com

Aerial photographs reproduced under licence from Simmons Aerofilms Limited
Historical Ordnance Survey maps reproduced under licence from Homecheck.co.uk

Printed and bound in England

Front Cover: **BUXTON, CRESCENT HOTEL 1932** 85218t
The colour-tinting in this image is for illustrative purposes only,
and is not intended to be historically accurate

Every attempt has been made to contact copyright holders of illustrative material.
We will be happy to give full acknowledgement in future editions for any items not credited.
Any information should be directed to The Francis Frith Collection.

AS WITH ANY HISTORICAL DATABASE, THE FRANCIS FRITH ARCHIVE IS CONSTANTLY BEING
CORRECTED AND IMPROVED, AND THE PUBLISHERS WOULD WELCOME INFORMATION ON
OMISSIONS OR INACCURACIES

FRANCIS FRITH'S
TOWN & CITY
MEMORIES

CONTENTS

THE MAKING OF AN ARCHIVE

FRANCIS FRITH, Victorian founder of the world-famous photographic archive, was a devout Quaker and a highly successful Victorian businessman. By 1860 he was already a multi-millionaire, having established and sold a wholesale grocery business in Liverpool. He had also made a series of pioneering photographic journeys to the Nile region. The images he returned with were the talk of London. An eminent modern historian has likened their impact on the population of the time to that on our own generation of the first photographs taken on the surface of the moon.

Frith had a passion for landscape, and was as equally inspired by the countryside of Britain as he was by the desert regions of the Nile. He resolved to set out on a new career and to use his skills with a camera. He established a business in Reigate as a specialist publisher of topographical photographs.

Frith lived in an era of immense and sometimes violent change. For the poor in the early part of Victoria's reign work was a drudge and the hours long, and ordinary people had precious little free time. Most had not travelled far beyond the boundaries of their own town or village. Mass tourism was in its infancy during the 1860s, but during the next decade the railway network and the establishment of Bank Holidays and half-Saturdays gradually made it possible for the working man and his family to enjoy holidays and to see a little more of the world. With characteristic business acumen, Francis Frith foresaw that these new tourists would enjoy having souvenirs to commemorate their days out. He began selling photo-souvenirs of seaside resorts and beauty spots, which the Victorian public pasted into treasured family albums.

Frith's aim was to photograph every town and village in Britain. For the next thirty years he travelled the country by train and by pony and trap, producing fine photographs of seaside resorts and beauty spots that were keenly bought by millions of Victorians.

THE RISE OF FRITH & CO

Each photograph was taken with tourism in mind, the small team of Frith photographers concentrating on busy shopping streets, beaches, seafronts, picturesque lanes and villages. They also photographed buildings: the Victorian and Edwardian eras were times of huge building activity, and town halls, libraries, post offices, schools and technical colleges were springing up all over the country. They were invariably celebrated by a proud Victorian public, and photo souvenirs – visual records – published by F Frith & Co were sold in their hundreds of thousands. In addition, many new commercial buildings such as hotels, inns and pubs were photographed, often because their owners specifically commissioned Frith postcards or prints of them for re-sale or for publicity purposes.

In order to gain some understanding of the scale of Frith's business one only has to look at the catalogue issued by Frith & Co in 1886: it runs to some 670 pages. By 1890 Frith had created the greatest specialist photographic publishing company in the world, with over 2,000 stockists! The picture on the right shows the Frith & Co display board on the wall of the stockist at Ingleton in the Yorkshire Dales (left of window). Beautifully constructed with a mahogany frame and gilt inserts, it displayed a dozen scenes.

POSTCARD BONANZA

The ever-popular holiday postcard we know today took many years to appear, and F Frith & Co was in the vanguard of its development. Postcards became a hugely popular means of communication and sold in their millions. Frith's company took full advantage of this boom and soon became the major publisher of photographic view postcards.

Francis Frith died in 1898 at his villa in Cannes, his great project still growing. His sons Eustace and Cyril continued their father's monumental task, expanding the number of views offered to the public and recording more and more places in Britain, as the coasts and countryside were opened up to mass travel. The archive Frith created continued in business for another seventy years. By 1970 it contained over a third of a million pictures of 7,000 cities, towns and villages. The massive photographic record Frith has left to us stands as a living monument to a special and very remarkable man.

This book shows Buxton as it was photographed by this world-famous archive at various periods in its development over the past 150 years. Every photograph was taken for a specific commercial purpose, which explains why the selection may not show every aspect of the town landscape. However, the photographs, compiled from one of the world's most celebrated archives, provide an important and absorbing record of your town.

BUXTON IN HISTORY

BUXTON, in the High Peak of Derbyshire has been an inland resort for more than 2000 years. The town sits in a bowl at 300 metres above sea level surrounded by hills which rise to 500 metres. Nowadays the immediate hills around the town are heavily wooded but this was not always so, early travellers found a barren and inhospitable terrain which had to be traversed before reaching Buxton. Dr Hall, writing in 1863 said: "...A few generations back, the country for many miles round Buxton still remained so bleak and, with a few exceptions, so dreary that but for the rheumatic invalid seeking benefit from its waters, and the comforts of its inns and numerous boarding-houses, it possessed comparatively few attractions for strangers...". But reports of miraculous cures caused early travellers to brave the hardships in search of relief from the warm medicinal waters which rise from springs located in the present Crescent at a constant temperature of 82°F (27.5°C).

VIEW FROM THE SLOPES 1932 85213

The Crescent was designed by John Carr of York and built for the 5th Duke of Devonshire between 1780 and 1784. The warm springs emerge in the area of the left-hand side of the picture and the Crescent was built in a low-lying grove of trees. The River Wye flows around the outer rim of the building. Part of the Quadrant can be seen on the extreme right, the Palace Hotel behind the Crescent and the Devonshire Royal Hospital, now the University of Derby, Buxton, with domed roof to the left.

Above: THE PUMP ROOM 1914 67572
Across the road the half-round windows, on the ground floor of the single-storey building on the right, show the site of the original Roman Bath, in constant use from that time. Beyond is the Hall of 1573.

Right: THE SQUARE 1903 49875
Designed by John White and Son and built 1804-06 for the 5th Duke of Devonshire.

Far Right: MARKET PLACE 1894 34228

BUXTON IN HISTORY

In 1700 Charles Leigh, Doctor of Physick at Oxford, wrote that he had seen remarkable instances of the effects of Buxton water on persons who arrived on crutches and returned, unaided, on foot to Manchester. Daniel Defoe, travelling on his 'Tour through the Whole Island of Great Britain' in the early 18th century, said that he must give praise to the warm springs for their medicinal virtue and the wonderful cures which had been effected by them in "...rheumatick, scorbutic and scrofulous distempers, aches of the joints, nervous pains, and also in scurvy and leprous maladies...".

But Buxton was not just celebrated for its miraculous water. From the 16th century writers referred to the wholesome and pure air in Buckstones, adding that its pureness is most profitable to all. Many subsequent accounts have recorded the particularly dry, bracing and stimulating character of the air. So Buxton has enjoyed, through time, a reputation for its natural mineral water, its mountainous situation and the salubrity of its air.

The earliest evidence of man in Buxton suggests occupation in an area close by the natural springs during the Mesolothic (or Middle Stone Age) period, about 5000 BC into the Neolithic or New Stone Age (3500-1800 BC). Buxton was a Roman Spa of some importance, standing on the junction of at least five roads with evidence of three baths and a shrine. The Romans used the name 'Aquae' for only two centres with a natural thermal water, Aquae Sulis for Bath in Somerset and Aquae Arnemetiae for Buxton. Arnemetia was a minor Celtic deity who became a Roman goddess, which suggests an earlier Celtic connection. A votive find at the site of the main bath in 1975 has identified coins dating from 100 to 400 AD, and Romano-British farming settlements around the town suggest activity at Buxton for the whole of the period of occupation in Britain.

BUXTON IN HISTORY

Buxton's fame rests on its natural thermal water. Here are the Hot or Thermal Baths where natural mineral water was heated to temperatures of about 35°C (95°F). In addition to the natural baths there was a cold plunging bath and an iron-rich chalybeate (pronounced Kali-be-at) water drunk by those with anaemic conditions.

The fame of Buxton as a Medieval spa grew and in Tudor times was greatly enhanced by the visits of Mary Queen of Scots who came to take the waters for her various illnesses, including rheumatism and a recurring pain in the side. Her custodian, the 6th Earl of Shrewsbury, built the Hall (now the Old Hall Hotel) in order to house the captive queen and enclose the bath. Queen Mary came on at least five occasions between 1573 and 1584, as did prominent members of the Elizabethan court including Robert Dudley, the Earl of Leicester, and Lord Burghley, the Lord Treasurer. The Earl of Shrewsbury's wife, Bess of Hardwick, who was a good businesswoman, took

St Anne's Well was described as one of the Seven Wonders of the Peak by a number of writers including Charles Cotton and Thomas Hobbes, the philosopher and tutor to the Cavendish family. Hobbes' book 'De Mirabilibus Pecci'- the Wonders of the Peak - published in 1678, describes:

'Unto St Ann the Fountain sacred is: With waters hot and cold its sources rise, And in its Sulphur veins there's med'cine lies. This cures the palsied members of the Old. And cherishes the Nerves grown stiff and cold. Crutches the Lame unto its brink convey, Returning the ungrates fling them away. The Barren hither to be fruitful comes, And without help of Spouse, go pregnant home'.

With such publications came increased interest requiring the area of lower Buxton around the baths to be developed by successive Dukes of Devonshire through the 17th and 18th centuries. This culminated in the impressive investment of the 5th Duke who commissioned the Crescent and stables, the Square, Hall Bank and St John's Church, all between 1780 and 1811.

In Higher Buxton the Eagle Hotel, formerly the Eagle and Child, was completely rebuilt by the 4th Duke in 1760. It overlooks the market place, an open area from medieval times, though Buxton did not obtain a market charter until 1813.

The Georgian Spa of Buxton enjoyed modest success, but never really rivalled Bath as a fashionable centre for resorting. The more spectacular growth came in the 60 years from 1850, when the town became a busy and prosperous centre for water medicine and an inland holiday resort. This coincides with Francis Frith's most prolific period of photography and many of the images in this book capture the bustling nature of the town at this time. After the First World War Buxton had to reposition itself in the leisure market and Frith photographs from the 1920s onward record the various changing fashions in leisure in the resort.

advantage of this patronage at a time when the secular holiday was just beginning to emerge. Buxton's reputation was further enhanced by the writing of Dr John Jones, whose book 'The Benefit of the Auncient Bathes of Buckstones' of 1572 was the first to be published on the medical properties of the waters. In the 17th century,

FROM THE AIR

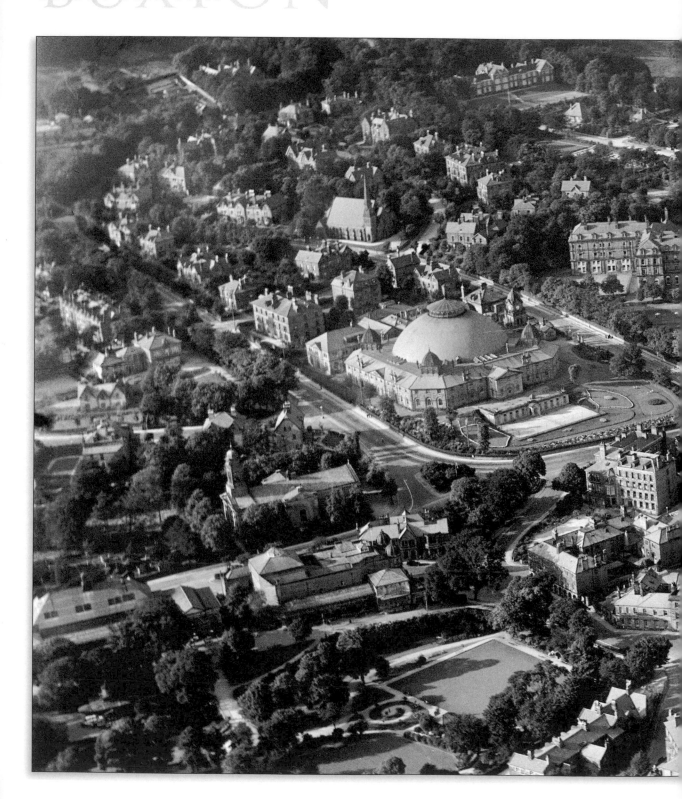

BUXTON FROM THE AIR 1930 AF34105

GROWTH OF AN INLAND RESORT

Right: BUXTON FROM SOLOMON'S TEMPLE 1894 34233

Compare this view with that in view 1456. The Palace Hotel is prominent in both views in the centre background, but the later view shows extensive residential growth on the left or the west side of the town. The curve of buildings in the centre is Broad Walk and behind it expansion in Higher Buxton. College Road in the right foreground is indicative of the spreading tentacles of residential growth at this time.

Below: PAVILION GARDENS C1873 5208

This is a view over the Pavilion Gardens lower lake showing part of Cavendish Villas, the four-bay building to the right. The double-fronted house on the left was built in 1871 as G F Barnard's private residence. To the left of this may be seen the bottom of Hall Bank where a new hotel, The Burlington, is under construction.

Below Centre: BUXTON FROM SOLOMON'S TEMPLE C1862 1456

Below Right: THE CRESCENT 1902 48183

A view of the Crescent showing the Natural Baths (left wing) and the Hot Baths (right wing), both remodelled in 1851-54 by Henry Currey. On the right, behind the Hot Baths is the Quadrant (1853-64) and behind that, the end facades of the two stations can be seen. The left station is the LNWR and the right the MR.

GROWTH OF AN INLAND RESORT

IN 1848 there were fewer than 1,500 residents in Buxton with eight hotels, eight inns and about 100 households offering accommodation to visitors in the season. By 1905 a population of over 10,000 was hosting more than 4,000 visitors each week in 27 hotels and more than 300 lodging houses or apartments. Phenomenal growth in just 60 years was brought about by a rich combination of factors. Doctors promoted the use of the natural mineral waters for a range of conditions chiefly, but not wholly, associated with rheumatic disease. People coming to take the water treatment would stay at a hotel or in a lodging house, consult the local medical specialist and embark on a course of treatment. In between episodes of treatment they would look for entertainment. Many arrived in town with their family, turning the visit into a holiday and a variety of different leisure activities were needed. The town grew on two fronts: as a medical centre and as an inland resort. It was driven forward in the earlier 19th century by the agents of the Duke of Devonshire who was the principal landowner. Investment by the Devonshire Estate in new hot and natural baths between 1851 and 1854 provided an early incentive to local townsmen and the Quadrant, a commercial and residential road behind the Crescent, soon followed. Sir Joseph Paxton, the 6th Duke's designer and confidant, laid out Buxton Park for fashionable housing and some substantial villas were erected. Lodging houses were built on Terrace Road and Hall Bank, the two roads which connected the fashionable

GROWTH OF AN INLAND RESORT

PAVILION GARDENS AND BROAD WALK C1873 5207

This view shows Grosvenor Terrace, built in 1864 as lodging houses.

GROWTH OF AN INLAND RESORT

lower town, baths and Crescent with the old higher town and Market Place.

Buxton was fortunate in being developed as an estate town, since careful attention was paid to the necessary services. A Gas Light and Coke Company was formed in 1851, and piped water was fed to certain parts of the town by the Devonshire Estate. The installation of a new sewerage and drainage system coincided with the formation of the first local authority, the Buxton Local Board, in 1859 - by which time the town had a water works owned and operated by the Devonshire Estate. These amenities were essential in a town which prided itself on its healthful clean air and medicinal water.

BROAD WALK C1955 B263019

Such was the character of the gravelled pedestrian Broad Walk with its Italianate villas, attractive lamp standards and bollards that it regularly appeared in the albums of commercial photographers well into the 20th century. In the foreground, Grosvenor House has a two-storey consulting and waiting rooms designed by the architects Barry Parker and Raymond Unwin in 1901-02 for Dr W Tweed Hannah.

GROWTH OF AN INLAND RESORT

GROWTH OF AN INLAND RESORT

GROWTH OF AN INLAND RESORT

PAVILION GARDENS AND BROAD WALK C1873 5209

Here we can some of the delights of the gardens flanked by fashionable housing. Seen from the left is Holly Bank, Milton House and Cavendish House, beyond which may be seen Derby House. All of these properties were operating as private lodging houses in 1873 providing high quality rooms for the visitor. Broad Walk had extended to more detached and semi-detached villas by 1875 and provided a link between the baths in the Crescent and the cold water Tonic Bath on Bath Road.

GROWTH OF AN INLAND RESORT

The cotton boom of the 1850s helped to increase the number of visitors as the town began to improve its facilities, but it was the arrival of the railways which stimulated accelerating growth, not only in staying guests, but also in a new kind of visitor, the day-tripper. The London and North Western (LNWR) and Midland Railways (MR) both officially opened their station in June 1863. The MR, supported by Sir Joseph Paxton had driven a route from Rowsley through stunning scenery and over Monsal Head viaduct, a remarkable feat of engineering. The LNWR came in from the northerly town of Whaley Bridge. Though in competition with each other, the railway companies were obliged by the Devonshire Estate to build uniform facades to their stations, which stood side by side.

From 1863, house building could commence in earnest, because not only would visitor numbers increase dramatically, but businessmen from Manchester and its environs could move their family residence to the salubrious mountain air of Buxton and take advantage of a 40-minute journey to the office. From this time, a large number of substantial villas were built either for single

GROWTH OF AN INLAND RESORT

THE CRESCENT C1870 5195

Views such as this tell us much about the growth of the town. The building on the left of the Crescent is the Old Hall Hotel behind which is the Devonshire Hospital, at that time functioning as part hospital, part stables before its conversion fully into hospital use. Behind the Devonshire Hospital is the very early development of Devonshire Park, where there are few houses as yet and the Wesleyan Church of 1873 is yet to be built. To the left of Devonshire Park can be seen Manchester Road and the limited development of the Buxton Park, including the Leewood Hotel, built in 1864.

family occupation, or more often to be let as apartments or run as lodging house businesses.

Broad Walk is a fine example of this kind of investment. It was developed between 1861 and the early 1870s to become one of the most fashionable Victorian terraces in the town, in an unrivalled position overlooking the Hall Gardens, which were to become the finest example of Victorian Gardenesque in town and an unrivalled amenity. In 1861, Broad Walk was laid out as the new Cavendish Terrace with the first three houses, known as Cavendish Villas, erected as lodging houses for Mr G F Barnard, a local wine and spirit merchant.

There followed a further set of lodging houses known as Grosvenor Terrace owned by wealthy hotelier, Brian Bates, among others.

By 1868 there were 15 properties including Milton, Cavendish and Derby Houses, Lake Villas, Stanley Villas, Dalton House and Cambridge Villas. The earlier houses exhibit the Italianate features much favoured by the Duke of Devonshire's architect, Henry Currey, the later designs are most probably by the local architect, Robert Rippon Duke.

GROWTH OF AN INLAND RESORT

A great deal of house building took place from the early 1860s in both Higher and Lower Buxton, as demand for substantial houses for letting and as lodging houses increased markedly. The 20 years to 1880 saw a 125% increase in houses from 458 to 1,030, and the number of roads more than doubled to 42. Many building plots were laid out by the Devonshire Estate surveyor, R R Duke, on the western side of the town to take advantage of the prevailing westerly wind. Devonshire Park was developed for fashionable residential housing earlier than the Buxton Park, which had been laid out in the 1850s by Paxton but few plots had sold. These two residential parks were separated by the main road to Manchester. R R Duke designed two houses for the estate in Devonshire Park; the stonemason, Henry Vickers, developed two plots; and the local photographer Barrowclough W Bentley, who must have made the acquaintance of Francis Frith, also bought a plot of land there. The Wesley Methodists built a chapel in the centre of the park, on the corner of Devonshire and Marlborough roads in 1873, '...a large and noble building in the Gothic style with a tower and an octagonal spire...'.

The further development of Buxton Park in the 1880s led to high-class residential growth around the south western edge of the town, linking St John's Road and Green Lane and incorporating new roads such as Burlington (completed 1890), College (1892), Spencer (1895) and Robertson (1897). As the resort reached its apogee, the early 20th century saw some outstanding houses in the Arts and Crafts and Cheshire Domestic Revival styles, built as family homes by wealthy businessmen and designed by respected regional architects. Families such as the Bengers of Benger's Foods, the Seebohm shipping family, McDougal the flour millers and Digby Johnson the insurers, commissioned architects such as Charles Heathcote of Manchester, Huon A Matear of Liverpool and local man William Radford Bryden to build individual detached houses set in a small estate. Barry Parker and Raymond Unwin, later to become nationally known for their work in the Garden City movement, had an office in the Quadrant and designed a number of outstanding Arts and Crafts style houses in Buxton.

GROWTH OF AN INLAND RESORT

THE CRESCENT 1896 37851

Compare this with 5195, pages 24-25. In less than 30 years both Devonshire and Buxton Parks are complete, and Corbar Road (in the lee of Corbar Woods) is composed of residential housing. The Devonshire Hospital is now fully converted and has its magnificent domed roof.

GROWTH OF AN INLAND RESORT

In Higher Buxton, a great deal of lower-middle class housing was built, often three-storey and presenting a facade of solid Victorian respectability. These houses, quite large by today's standards, were often built in short terraces, with small front gardens and a yard at the rear but, in common with many other houses in Buxton, they were designed to take in visitors in the season. Behind these the working-class houses and cottages were carefully hidden away from the main thoroughfares. As a resort it was desirable to present a tidy and reasonably prosperous-looking facade to the visitors as they drove along the main roads of the town. Francis Frith was, of course, interested in taking views which would make good souvenirs, so whilst we may identify some of the better class of housing in his photographs, he did not record the more modest stock, important though that is to the history of this inland resort.

By 1905 the number of roads had again doubled to 84 and there were 2,000 houses, a number of which provided lodgings for the influx of more than 4,000 visitors each week. These halcyon days would not return after the First World War (1914-18) but the town always strove to do what it was best at - attract and entertain the visitor. In the 1920s and 30s successful efforts were made to establish Buxton as a conference centre, and in the 1940s and 50s, the town prospered as an inland resort providing a wide range of entertainment. With the largest ballroom in the Peak District, it was able to attract nationally known 'big bands' such as those of Ted Heath, Joe Loss, and Victor Sylvester. Frith recorded all these changes.

THE CRESCENT C1955 B263008

A much quieter place than 50 years previously.

CRESCENT HOTEL 1902 48184

By this time the east wing had been renamed the Crescent Hotel. In the 1970s the whole of this wing was used as offices for Derbyshire County Council and the assembly room on the first floor became the town's public library. On the right can be seen the Hot Baths after its new stone frontage had been added in 1900.

HOTELS AND COMMERCE

OF Buxton's Hotels, the oldest by far is the Old Hall Hotel. The original 'Derbyshire square house' of 1573 has been extended considerably over time, but recent investigations have discovered that much of the original building remains within the hotel.

The Grove Hotel, at the junction of the Quadrant and Spring Gardens, started life as a coffee house and dates to the 1770s. It gained prominence as a coaching inn when the Manchester road was diverted around the present Quadrant and up Yeomans Lane (Terrace Road). The colonnading was added around 1883 by the landlord, Joseph Whalley. The George Hotel was built at roughly the same time as the Grove and received passing trade from the Manchester to Derby turnpike which at that time passed the frontage of the hotel.

The Georgian Crescent has been used as hotel accommodation for much of its life. Originally it contained two hotels, the St Anne's

Left: Spring Gardens c1862 1462

The Royal Hotel on the left was built on the site of the former Angel Inn. The wording 'Winster Place' can still just be made out in the stonework at the eastern end of the building. The chief financier of the project was Andrew Brittlebank, a solicitor from the township of Winster. The building has passed through the hands of many owners and was taken over in 1914 by Buxton Lime Firms Company as offices. The licence continued during this period as the Royal Vaults bar until its closure in 1956. From 1926 the building was used as offices for Imperial Chemical Industries (ICI) and renamed the Royal Exchange, continuing as such until the early 1980s. Today it has become an integral part of the Spring Gardens Shopping Centre, providing several shops.

Below Left: Crescent Hotel, Dining Room 1902 48188

This is the Assembly Room designed by John Carr with decorative plaster ceiling and chandeliers. The doors at the rear of this view originally lead off to coffee and card rooms.

Below Centre: Palace Hotel c1885 B263506

Designed by the Duke of Devonshire's architect, Henry Currey.

Below: Palace Hotel 1923 74135

and the Great, with six town houses in the centre. By 1807 these town houses, one of which was used by the 5th Duke, had been converted into the Centre Hotel.

The Royal Hotel in Spring Gardens was built in 1849-51 and was designed by the Sheffield Architect, Samuel Worth. Buxton's foremost architect, Robert Rippon Duke, moved to the town from Hull in 1849, and his first job was to superintend the erection of this hotel. Built with a convex frontage to contrast with the concave front of the Crescent, the hotel was very imposing, standing in an area which was relatively uncrowded by today's standards. Extensive alterations and enlargement of the hotel took place in 1882 to the

designs of Robert Duke, and the building was renamed the Royal Hotel and Wine stores. The work included the addition of an octagonal billiard room and a lawn tennis ground at the rear.

The arrival of the railway brought ever more visitors and the building of the largest hotel in the town, the Palace. It was built as a speculative venture from 1866 to 1868 and was originally known as the Buxton Hotel. The project had a very shaky beginning and came close to financial collapse with the severe loss of confidence nationally in joint-stock companies. The hotel eventually prospered, however, and was increased in size in 1887, with the addition of a large dining room at the rear of the hotel which was designed by Robert Rippon Duke. The

Left: ASHWOOD PARK HOTEL 1923 *74132*

Seen here from the A6 Bakewell road, the building was bought in 2000 by the nation-wide public house chain, J D Wetherspoon, and it has reverted to its original name of Wye Bridge House.

Below: THE RAILWAY HOTEL 1923 *74137*

The Railway Hotel on Bridge Street was built in 1864 by the Chesterfield Brewery Company and has changed little externally over the years.

west wing of the hotel stands back slightly from the main building and was designed by Duke in partnership with William Bryden in 1888.

The Leewood Hotel in Buxton Park was converted from three private houses and opened in 1864. The proprietor was Brian Bates who also ran the Old Hall and Royal Hotels. Another hotel which owes its existence to the coming of the railway was the Midland, situated at the northern end of Ashwood Park. It was built in the 1870s and was originally named Wye Bridge House. It was purchased by Buxton Corporation in 1921, and by 1925 was known as the Ashwood Park Hotel.

The Burlington Hotel at the foot of Hall Bank replaced an earlier Georgian property and was another of Robert Rippon Duke's designs. Built in 1874 at a cost of £4,320, the hotel was later named the Savoy and was used as a training hotel for the brewery trade. The building uses a different style of window for each storey and, although it is now private flats, the name 'Burlington' can still be been in the stonework at first floor level.

The giant Empire Hotel was built in the Park 1902-3 by Spiers and Pond at a cost of £150,000. It was very luxurious and opened only in the season but had a short commercial life. It was used as an annexe to the Granville Military Hospital during the First World War and afterwards as a discharge depot for Canadian troops. Squatters inhabited the empty hotel after the Second World War but were evicted in 1949. The building was demolished in 1964.

HOTELS AND COMMERCE

With increases in both population and numbers of visitors to the town, provision had to be made for their shopping requirements. Although there are shops in higher Buxton, on High Street and the Market Place, the major commercial centre is Spring Gardens in the lower town. Originally known as Town Street or Sheffield Road, it was developed into a busy shopping street selling, among other things, tourist gifts. Here you could buy ornaments made of Blue John, Ashford Black Marble and Derbyshire Spar - locally mined stones which were worked in the Petrifaction and Spar shops.

The number and type of shops in Spring Gardens has altered greatly over the years but the architecture on either side remains largely unchanged. An increase in traffic through the street led to calls for pedestrianisation which was completed in 1997.

Right: SPRING GARDENS 1923 74118

The convex curve of the Royal Hotel building is seen just left of centre. Beyond that is the banner of the popular and long-running Miller's Restaurant. On the right is The London County Westmister & Parr's Bank.

Left: SPRING GARDENS C1955 B263004

Seen from the Slopes this view shows the colonnading curving around the front of the Grove Hotel and into Spring Gardens which remains in place today. The left half of the ground floor of the Royal Hotel building is occupied by a branch of the Burgon's national grocery chain.

Far Left: TERRACE ROAD & SPRING GARDENS 1932 85216

On the left can be seen the Hot Baths with iron and glass colonnading. The relatively light traffic at this time did not need regulating with traffic lights. A solitary policeman was quite sufficient.

DERBYSHIRE COUNTY MAP

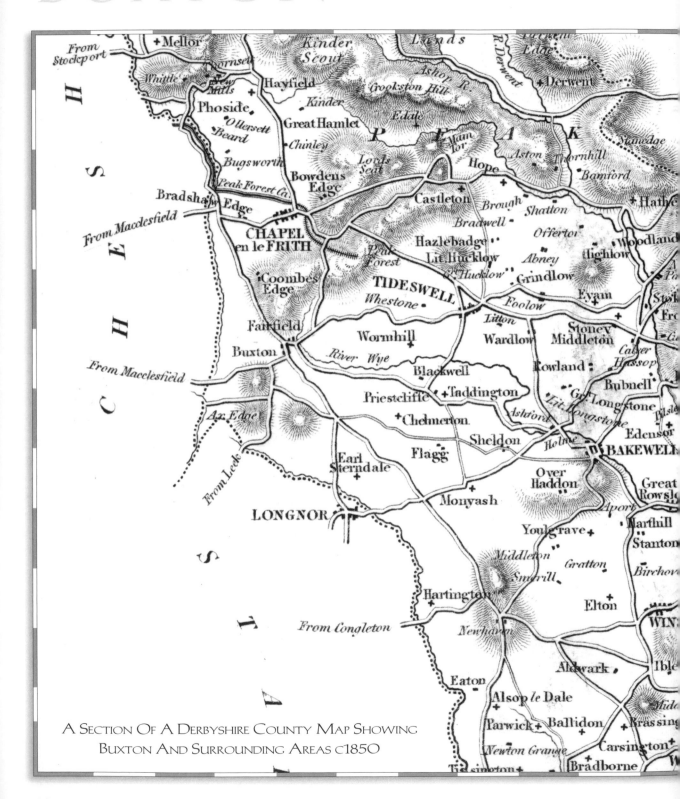

A SECTION OF A DERBYSHIRE COUNTY MAP SHOWING
BUXTON AND SURROUNDING AREAS c1850

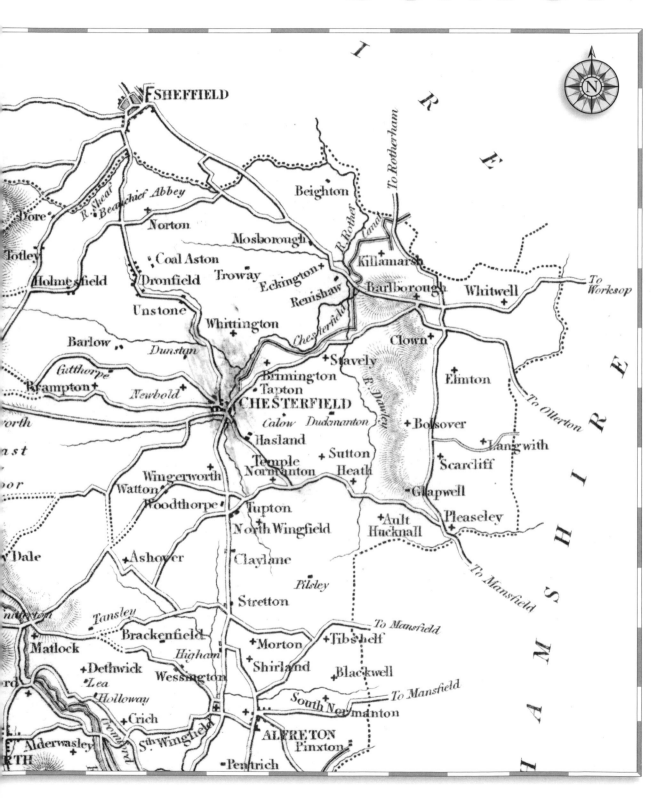

Pavilion Gardens

The Crescent and Bandstand c1864 2137

PAVILION GARDENS

THE origins of the Pavilion Gardens lie in the tradition of the town band which entertained the many visitors. It played in the Crescent in a Promenade Room and under a wooden umbrella-like structure outside. Up to the late 1860s the 7th Duke supported the band at his own expense, but increasingly he wished to see the town become more self-sufficient. He progressively reduced his donation, offering about a fifth of the £500 annual cost of running the band, the shortfall being made up from public donations and subscriptions. Towards the end of the decade this method of funding became inadequate, and the duke was prompted to suggest the setting up of a private company which would provide pleasure gardens and the band, paid for by an entrance fee.

Thus it was that the Buxton Improvements Company was formed. In 1870 the duke donated 12 acres of the Hall Gardens to the company with the stipulation that they enclose the area and build a pavilion or 'winter garden' to attract the paying customer. The gardens in front of the hall had until this time been open freely to the public but the new company was to undertake a complete re-landscaping of the grounds.

The architect chosen to landscape the grounds and build the glass and iron pavilion was Edward Milner who had trained under the architect of London's Crystal Palace, Joseph Paxton.

The gardens were laid out in conjunction with Milner's son, Henry Ernest in an undulating style designed to provide areas of light and shade and different levels of planting. The River Wye was dammed in several places creating cascades and waterfalls. Bridges were built over the river - the most substantial of which, made in stone and iron, still remains today below the Pavilion Central Hall. The makers' name - H Bayley Son & Co. Manchester - is cast into the bridge.

The Winter Gardens and grounds were opened to the public on 11 May 1871. The Pavilion building was about 400 feet in length

BUXTON

Pavilion Gardens

Hall Gardens c1862 1463

PAVILION GARDENS

HALL GARDENS C1865 2793

with a square central hall for concerts and a wing on either side for promenading in wet weather. In front of the building, a terrace walk was built for promenading during dry conditions. The attraction was an instant success, bringing a great many visitors to the town, so much so that by as early as October 1872 pressure was being put on the company to make extensions to the buildings to provide more facilities for visitors.

There can be little question that the Improvements Company was proud of the Gardens and its popularity, and particularly the band under the spirited direction of Mr Julian Adams, whose popular concerts were the greatest cause of overcrowding in the central hall of the Pavilion. The concerts were exceptionally well attended and it was quite usual to see some of the audience sitting on the stone sills outside the concert room, and standing crowds straining for a glimpse of the orchestra. The central hall was only 70 feet square, and during concerts in wet weather it was necessary for visitors who wished to move from one end of the Pavilion to the other to force themselves through the audience or else walk outside in the wind and rain. The Improvements Company were constantly being made aware of the problem both by visitors and residents and it was agreed that urgent action should be taken to remedy the situation.

The new concert hall was octagonal in shape and large enough to accommodate an audience of 2,000. In order to blend in with the existing Pavilion building it was built in a similar style, using iron and glass. The roof was extremely advanced for its time, being both domed and slated, with four windows spaced around the dome in order to light the interior from above. Work on the building commenced in April 1875, and the terrace in front of the pavilion had to be widened by nine feet to allow for the extra width of the new hall.

HALL GARDENS C1865 2795

PAVILION GARDENS

THE PAVILION c1871 5210

The Pavilion or Winter Gardens is seen here from the west end. It was built in 1871 to the designs of Edward Milner.

PAVILION GARDENS

PAVILION GARDENS c1871 5202

Pavilion Gardens

PAVILION GARDENS

The cast and wrought iron work was contracted to Messrs Rankin & Co of Liverpool. The whole building was complete by August 1876 - quite an achievement, but Victorian expectations were evidently very high if the number of letters to the local press complaining about the slow progress of the work are any guide. The building was opened on 30 August 1876 to great acclaim. Concern that the domed roof would distort the acoustic quality of the musical concerts were unfounded; architect Robert Duke had done his homework. The sound quality of the first concert, held on the opening day, was deemed to be excellent by all who attended. Set into the apex of the domed roof was a gas powered 'Sunlight Burner' to light the hall during evening performances. This burner is still in existence today but cannot be seen due to the introduction of a false ceiling at the level of the dome base.

During the construction of the Concert Hall, work was proceeding at the north west corner of the Improvement Company grounds to construct an outdoor skating rink. The fashion of roller skating was at its height at this time and the rink was built with a covered area to shelter the skaters during inclement weather. The rink, designed by R R Duke, was opened in the summer of 1876.

A further three acres of the Hall Gardens were transferred in 1876 from the Duke of Devonshire to the Improvements Company, increasing the land area controlled by the company to 15 acres.

PAVILION BRIDGE AND CENTRAL HALL c1871 B263505

This hall was used for concerts by the town band. Such was their popularity that the building was regularly overcrowded and audiences often spilled out onto the promenade.

PAVILION GARDENS

Expansion took place in 1879, when a further seven acres were conveyed from the Devonshire Estate at an annual chief rent of £76. This land extended from Jordan's Walk, which bisects the gardens, to Burlington Road. In 1890 the final piece of land was conveyed to the Improvements Company. This is the Serpentine Walks which continue along the river beyond Burlington Road.

Buxton now had much improved facilities for orchestral concerts and recitals but it still did not have a theatre, the previous theatre on Hall Bank having been demolished in 1854. Public demand for a theatre must have been recognised by the Improvements Company, and in 1887 the directors were discussing the possibility of providing one within the pleasure grounds. Under their Memorandum of Association the Company was not permitted to erect such a building and it was necessary to reconstitute the company with extended powers to allow for the construction of the new building and any others it might choose to erect. Consequently, the Buxton Improvements Company ceased to exist on 27 March 1888 and was replaced with a new company named the Buxton Gardens Company.

PAVILION GARDENS

PROMENADING CORRIDOR, THE PAVILION c1871 5211

The local architect, William Radford Bryden was chosen to design the theatre. He had established his reputation as a creative and competent architect in 1886 with his first significant Buxton building, the Union Club (now the Old Clubhouse). He went on to design further impressive architecture in the town including The Hawthorns, Burlington Road (1896), Milnthorp Homes (1905) and Buxton Hospital (1912).

The choice of site for the new theatre is puzzling. It stands behind the Pavilion with its roof structure clearly visible from the Gardens promenade and spoiling the airy and light impression which was originally intended for the Pavilion. The completed theatre opened for its first public performance on August 12 1889. The company did not want an opening ceremony but the moment was given recognition by the actor John Lawrence Toole (1830-1906), who made a small speech before the start of the play 'The Don' in which he played the leading role.

The name chosen for the theatre was The Entertainment Stage but it quickly became known as the New Theatre, later the Pavilion Theatre and, when the Opera House was opened, it was called the Old Theatre. It was a substantial improvement on all its predecessors and had a two-level auditorium seating 850 people. The building remained in use as a theatre for 25 years and then became a cinema known as the Hippodrome.

The roller skating rink underwent a change of use in 1906 when it became the fourth home of the Caledonian Curling Club. The sides of the rink were built up in order to retain a shallow layer of water which would freeze during the frosty weather. Three rinks were in use and the roofed-over area at the west end was still in place, giving a degree of shelter for spectators. In the 1920s it was converted to tennis courts and is now a car park.

In 1927, after a particularly poor year in terms of profit at both the Gardens and the Opera House, the Gardens Company entered into negotiations and the facilities were sold for £29,550 to the local authority in whose possession they remain today having undergone many minor renovations over the years. A major restoration of the Pavilion Gardens was completed in 2004. The project, under a £4.7m National Lottery Urban Parks Programme in conjunction with High Peak Borough Council, made many improvements to the park. Included in the renovation was the partial re-fencing of the perimeter, refurbishment of the Upper and Lower Lakes, installation of a new small gauge railway, restoration of Broad Walk and re-landscaping to reproduce the appearance of the 1871 Milner layout.

THE PAVILION C1871 2796

The local architect, Robert Rippon Duke, devised plans to build a new concert hall to be situated at the west end of the Pavilion.

Pavilion Gardens

A BAND CONCERT IN THE PAVILION GARDENS C1871 5198

The landscaping of Edward and Henry Milner included the building of a bandstand within the grounds. This picture shows that these concerts were popular with the visitors. Although demolished many years ago, the base of the stand can still be seen today in its original position. A replacement bandstand, based on the original design but much larger, was built in the grounds in 1998.

PAVILION GARDENS

Right: PAVILION GARDENS c1871 5197

Below: THE CONCERT HALL 1932 85222

This view shows the hall in its original form. The two buildings projecting from its west end are the Board Room and, at the extreme west, with the lower roof is the Smoking Room. Note the ornate windows in the domed roof. Copies of these windows were cast and re-introduced in the dome during the restoration of 1993.

Below Right: THE ISLAND, HALL GARDENS c1862 1467

BUXTON

PAVILION GARDENS

THE OPERA HOUSE 1923 74133

The new Opera House opened in 1903. It was built at the north-eastern corner of the gardens adjacent to the main entrance. The Gardens Company chose the prolific theatre architect, Frank Matcham, to design the building which, despite being built into a rather cramped and irregular area, was erected in a relatively short time and to very high specifications. A cantilever supporting design for the Dress and Upper circles obviated the need for supporting pillars and thus a good view of the stage could be obtained from all parts of the house. The Opera House was used as a cinema from the 1930s but, following a restoration in 1979, has been used as a theatre ever since. A recent and more thorough restoration, completed in spring 2001 with the aid of Heritage Lottery funding, has restored the building to its original splendour and it is a sight worth seeing for all visitors to the town.

Left: The Pavilion, Interior 1890 24734

Below: Pavilion Gardens, Boats on the Upper Lake 1932 85225
Rowing and paddle boats were a common sight on the upper lake from the 1930s through to the 1970s. Some of them endearingly carried identifying names, the two paddle boats in this view are called Hamish and Paddy.

Bottom: Pavilion Gardens c1872 B263502

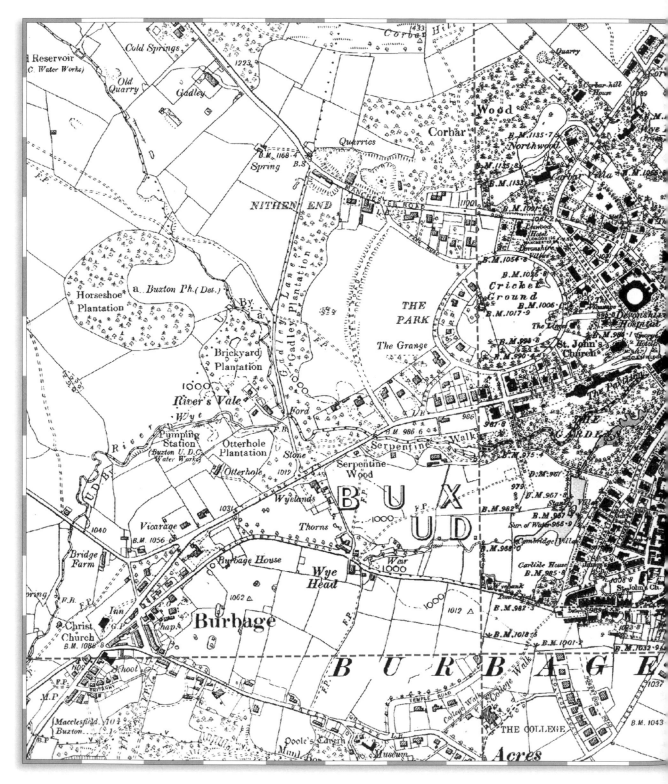

AN ORDNANCE SURVEY MAP SHOWING BUXTON AND SURROUNDING AREAS 1879-1898

LAYOUT OF THE NATURAL AND HOT BATHS FROM ROBERTSON'S BUXTON GUIDE 1861

GROUND PLAN OF THE NATURAL BATHS

SOUTH FRONT

References to Ground Plan of Natural Baths.

A. Ladies' public bath.
B. Women's charity bath.
C. Men's charity bath.
D. Gentlemen's public baths.
E. Gentlemen's private baths.
F. Ladies' Private baths.
G. Dressing-boxes
H. Dressing-rooms.
I. Gentlemen's corridor and waiting-room.
K. Ladies' do.

L. Lobby.
M. Water-closets.
N. Douche-closets.
O. Furnace-room.
P. Drying-room.
Q. Store-room.
R. Bath-keeper's office.
S. Drinking-well.
T. St Anne's drinking-well
U. Cresent arcade.
V. West End of Cresent.
W. Dining-room.
X. Yard.

References to Ground Plan of Hot Baths.

A. Ladies' public bath.
B. Females' charity bath.
C. Men's charity bath.
D. Gentlemen's public bath.
E. Cold Swimming-bath.
F. Gentlemen's private baths.
G. Corridor and waiting-room.
H. Ladies' Private baths.
I. Corridor and waiting-room.
K. Dressing-rooms.
L. Dressing-boxes
M. Water-closets.

N. Douche-closets.
O. Ticket-office.
P. Bath-keeper's office.
Q. Store-rooms
R. Lobbies
S. Drying-rooms.
T. Boiler-house.
U. Engine-room.
V. Waiting-rooms.
W. Coal-place.
X. Yard.
Y. East End of Cresent.
Z. Arcaade
a. Cresent arcade.
b. Billiard-room.

GROUND PLAN OF THE HOT BATHS

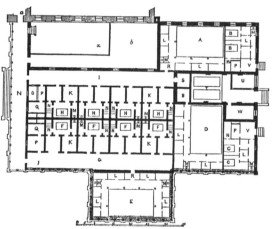

WATER CURE

DURING the 19th century, the reputation of Buxton as a centre for hydrotherapy was greatly enhanced by the work and writing of a number of prominent doctors. The most important of these was Dr W H Robertson who not only published on the medical efficacy of Buxton water, but also wrote the popular 'Guide to Buxton and the Peak of Derbyshire' which ran to 11 editions. Belief in the medicinal powers was fully exploited by doctors who devised increasingly complicated and sometimes bizarre treatments as the century proceeded. The main baths were situated at either side of the Crescent. On the west side, the original Natural Baths contained three large bathing pools, two for gentlemen and one for ladies, and charity baths. The Thermal or Hot Baths on the east side originally provided a public bath each for ladies and gentlemen, a cold swimming bath and four smaller private baths each for the two sexes. There were also four charity baths.

As treatment fashions changed, the use of smaller, private plunge baths increased and the layout of the buildings was modified a number of times. A Pump Room was situated in the Natural Baths where the natural mineral water and a chalybeate, or iron bearing water could be drunk. Later a separate Pump Room was built in the centre of the Crescent.

The doctors in Buxton, as at other centres such as Harrogate and Bath, believed in the special efficacy and healing value of the minerals in the natural water and its gaseous content. They would prescribe immersion for periods of time, sprays on the body, known as douches, showers and drinking of various quantities. The hydropathic movement, introduced into England from Austrian Silesia in the 1830s, did not require a natural mineral water, any water would do. What mattered was the treatment regime, diet, air and exercise so the use of

THE CRESCENT c1864 1457

It was possible, using the colonnade, to walk under cover from the Natural Baths and Pump Room on the left-hand side to the Hot Baths, seen on the extreme right as a single-storey building.

WATER CURE

Right: VIEW FROM THE SPA HOTEL 1932 85228

The Buxton Hydro was renamed the Spa Hotel in 1931. Situated on Hartington Road it had excellent views over its own tennis courts to the Pavilion Gardens beyond. This photograph shows the two-domed roofs by the local architect Robert Rippon Duke. On the right can be seen the Devonshire Hospital Dome of 1879-82 and on the left the octagonal roof of the Large Concert Hall (1876). Beyond this is the residential housing of St John's Road and Buxton Park.

Below Right: BUXTON HYDROPATHIC ESTABLISHMENT 1896 37856

Opened as Malvern House in 1866, this became the most successful hydro in town. Originally built for 40 patients, it was extended in 1890 and by 1905 had 260 rooms and luxurious public facilities including a grand ballroom.

Below: HADDON HALL HYDRO 1903 49874

wet and dry packs to the body, cold baths and the douche were re-inforced with a strict dietary and exercise regime. Hydropathic Hotels (hydros) sprang up in various parts of the country and some centres such as Matlock, Ilkley and Malvern embraced the technique fully. Buxton was much slower to welcome hydros - due undoubtedly to the firm line taken by Dr Robertson and his colleagues in their belief that only the natural mineral water could be efficaceous in the cure of rheumatism and other diseases. Hydros did eventually arrive in Buxton however and, perhaps inevitably, by the beginning of the 20th century treatments had been embraced by the wider science of water medicine called balneology and in an emerging specialism of hydrotherapy.

The reputation of the water treatment was enhanced by the Buxton Bath Charity, which formed the origins of the Devonshire Hospital. Poor people had been coming to take the waters since Elizabethan times, but in 1785 a set of rules were written which were to form the basis of the charity. Patients came from the Manchester cotton districts and elsewhere for a set number of weeks to receive board and lodging and free treatment. Many of the doctors gave their services free, and the charity was supported by collections taken from the better-off staying at the hotels and lodging houses. In 1858 the Bath Charity secured half the Georgian stables for conversion into a hospital and 20 years later the whole of the building was converted into a 300-bed hospital. The charity patients took water treatment in their own suite of baths adjacent to the Crescent, but in 1876 separate Charity Baths were erected and a separate drinking well provided for them in 1882.

WATER CURE

In 1905, 20 doctors were available to treat diseases of the circulatory, respiratory, locomoter and nervous systems as well as various rheumatic diseases, prescribing treatments using water, air, mud, electricity and combinations of these in a plethora of balneological cures for the paying patient. This level of activity continued up to the First World War, when Buxton's medical expertise was used in the war effort. Interest in this kind of treatment never regained its original level, though in the 1930s the three-week tonic cure was popular.

Although the baths did good service in the Second World War, they became increasingly commercially unviable, particularly after the 1948 National Health Act, and the baths eventually closed for medical treatment in the early 1960s.

Above: DEVONSHIRE ROYAL HOSPITAL FROM THE SLOPES c1955 B263005

Completed in 1882 by the architect R R Duke, the slated roof has a circumference of 138 feet (about 46m) which may be compared with St Paul's Cathedral at 112 feet (37m) and the Duomo in Florence at 139 feet (46m).

Left: THE CRESCENT c1955 B263020

This view shows part of the Crescent being used as an annexe to the Devonshire Royal Hospital. After the Act of 1948 treatment was available here for National Health patients until 1963.

Below: THE DOME OF THE DEVONSHIRE ROYAL HOSPITAL C1955 B263021

The iron framework resting on stone pillars can be clearly seen. Around the circumference is inscribed: '...One half of this building was given to the use of the sick poor by William Spencer Cavendish sixth Duke of Devonshire in the year 1859 and conveyed to the trustees as the Devonshire Hospital together with the pleasure grounds by William Cavendish, seventh Duke of Devonshire, in the year 1868. The remainder of the building was obtained in the year 1878 and the whole was internally reconstructed by the Governors of the Cotton Districts Convalescent Fund in the year 1881...'

Left: CRESCENT HOTEL 1932 85218

In the foreground are the Thermal or Hot Baths. The iron and glass canopy was renewed in 1910 after the front had been remodelled and the original canopy removed in 1900. The bath chairs are still operating at the time of this view. In the left distance can be seen the Pump Room, by then called St Anne's Well, still with its pepper pot domes, which were removed around 1937.

Spiritual Care

SPIRITUAL CURE

BURBAGE CHURCH c1862 1460

Henry Currey designed Christ Church in 1861. Edward Woollett Wilmot, the Duke of Devonshire's agent, was its strong promoter. This photograph was taken soon after it was completed.

WITH the great influx of visitors to the town came the need to care for spiritual, as well as physical, well-being. The mid 19th century was a time of great expansion of religious sects and denominations. Buxton saw no less than 11 new places of worship built for Anglican and Nonconformist worshippers. In the adjacent villages new churches were erected, notably the Anglican Christ Church in Burbage.

The establishment Anglicans were of the high church tradition, and sought to meet the needs of their growing congregation by extending St John's and building St James on Bath Road. Early in the 20th century they commissioned the wonderful Arts and Crafts Church of St Mary the Virgin on Dale Road by Derby architects, P H Currey and C C Thompson. The low Anglican Church tradition was met by Trinity Church on Hardwick Mount, entirely supported by Buxton's first modern solicitor, J W Taylor. He was its principal trustee for more than 50 years, insisting upon a plain and evangelical form of worship. The Roman Catholics built their church of St Anne on Terrace Road in 1861, a major benefactor being Samuel Grimshawe, wealthy land and mill owner of Errwood Hall in the Goyt Valley. Nonconformity was well represented, the Wesleyan Methodists extended their Market Place Chapel and built in Devonshire Park; the Primitive Methodists built a chapel and schoolroom on London Road.

The Congregational movement had a committed and wealthy following in town. The impressive church with tall spire on Hardwick Mount was

SPIRITUAL CARE

strongly promoted by Blackburn brewer, Henry Shaw, who lived at Corbar Hall. The architect was Henry Currey and it was built by the firm of R R Duke in 1861. Later, wealthy Congregational families in town included McDougal's flour millers and Vickery the Manchester metal dealer. Other denominations seemed to have a very small local following but relied on visitors to swell their congregation and collection plate. Amongst these were the Unitarians on Hartington Road and Catholic Apostolic Church on Hardwick Square South.

St Anne's Church interior 1890 24736

The small Anglican church on Bath Road dates to 1625 or earlier. This view of 1890 demonstrates the Anglo-Catholic tradition of that time in the Stations of the Cross on the walls and the cross, candle-sticks and vesper lights on the altar.

SPIRITUAL CURE

Left: St James's Church c1876 8821

Ever mindful of the need to keep up with growing congregations the Anglicans built the 750-seat St James the Great in 1871. It was designed by J Medland and Henry Taylor of Manchester.

Below Left: St John's Church interior 1890 24738

In 1896 the chancel of St John's was extended and remodelled resulting in the closure and resiting of the east entrances. This picture shows the interior of St John's just before the work commenced. The fixed pews gave way to chairs in about 1912. The alabaster font was designed by Henry Currey, the 7th Duke of Devonshire's architect.

Below: St John's Church c1862 1459

Dedicated in 1812, St John's was designed in a Neo-Classical Tuscan style by John White and Sons for the 5th Duke of Devonshire. It was at the centre of the fashionable life of the town and hence often photographed. There were originally entrances either side of the altar at the east end, as can be seen here.

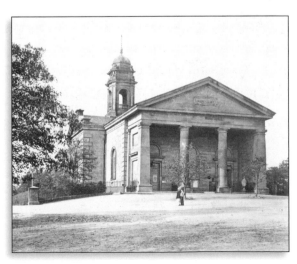

DAYS OUT

THE Pavilion Gardens provided outdoor and indoor amenities to entertain both locals and visitors to the town but what else was on offer to attract the attention of those with leisure time on their hands? The town had three other public parks, not on the scale of the Pavilion Gardens, but all with a charm of their own and were well patronised during the periods of Frith's recording of the town. The largest of these was Ashwood Park which was laid out as public recreation grounds from 1921.

The recreation ground at Heath Grove in Higher Buxton offered an open green space and a bowling green for the locals, whilst Sylvan Park provided an area of tranquillity at the eastern end of Spring Gardens. Both pieces of land were originally part of the Devonshire Estate and were leased at a peppercorn rent.

The sloping grassland area leading from Higher Buxton down to the Crescent was laid out in 1818 by Jeffrey Wyatt. Originally known as St Anne's Cliff it has been used for recreational purposes through time. The multi-level paths laid out on this hill were used to measure the degree of recovery of health in the invalids receiving treatments at the baths. More recently the area was renamed the Slopes, and after 1918 was chosen for the site of the town's war memorial.

The southern rim of the town bowl is crowned by Grin Low. This rocky limestone peak can be reached by a walk up through Grin Woods. The hill is crowned by the stone tower known today as Solomon's Temple, which was designed by local architect G E Garlick and opened in 1896. The tower replaced a previous folly which was reputedly built around 1835 to provide work for the unemployed of Buxton. The limestone in this area, being so close to the surface, was extensively exploited during the 18th and 19th centuries and limeburning was a major industry in the area. The remains of these primitive lime kilns and their spoil heaps are scattered all around this area.

ASHWOOD PARK MUNICIPAL BOWLING GREEN 1923 74127

This crown green is still in regular use today throughout the summer season. In the centre can be seen the ornamental bandstand which was demolished in the 1960s.

Days Out

Above: Ashwood Park c1955 B263011

This shows the park looking from the north. Behind the bridge in the centre of this view is the bowling pavilion. This has been replaced in recent times with a less decorative structure. Also included in the park were tennis courts and a childrens' play area. Several bridges span the river Wye along its course.

Above Right: Ashwood Park Cascade 1923 74131

Here we are looking northwards, showing the river and cascade. To the left can be seen the railway viaduct and the eastern end of Spring Gardens.

Left: THE SLOPES c1955 B263012

This view is looking north with the Palace Hotel, the east wing of the Crescent and the northern extremity of the Quadrant in the middle foreground. To the right of the centre of this view is one of the stone urns which still adorn the Slopes today. Following much vandalism over the years these have been recently restored.

DAYS OUT

Right: CORBAR WOODS 1915 *67578*

This wooded area to the north of the town was laid out and intersected with walks in the latter half of the 19th century and remain today a pleasant, if steep walk to the northern rim of the bowl within which the town sits. Good views can be had of the town from the top of Corbar Hill and of the moorland to the north over Lightwood Reservoir. Nithen Quarry in the western Corbar Woods was a source of high quality gritstone. Stone from this quarry was used to build the Town Hall on the Market Place in 1888. The disused quarry now operates as a residential caravan park.

Below Right: SOLOMON'S TEMPLE 1914 *67579*

The tower stands at 1440 feet above sea level on a Bronze-age barrow which was excavated in 1894.

Below: POOLE'S CAVERN GARDENS c1862 *1461*

On the left can be seen Redfern's Museum which contained a multitude of unrelated artefacts and curios which enhanced the attraction of a visit to the cave.

At the foot of Grin Low the popular showcave of Poole's Cavern has attracted visitors as far back as the 16th century when it is reputed that Mary, Queen of Scots explored the cave in 1573 during her period of captivity in the Hall at Buxton. The captive queen is said to have walked about 200 yards into the cavern, as far as a natural rock formation which was subsequently named Mary, Queen of Scots Pillar. Disturbance of the ground above the cavern during the intensive period of limeburning has released minerals into the water passing through the ground, enabling the formation of multi-coloured stalactites throughout the ceiling of the cave. The dripping of this mineral-laden water onto the ground beneath has lead to the slow build up of ground-based stalagmites. Famous among these are the 'poached egg' stalagmites so-called for their colouration.

GREAT NATURAL CURIOSITY.

POOLE'S CAVERN

ONCE THE RESORT
OF OUTLAWS :: ::

Effectively Illuminated

——— WITH ———

- Incandescent Gas. -

IN THE CAVERN may be seen POOLE'S CHAMBERS, the GREAT DOME, the CASCADE, the FLITCH OF BACON, the OLD ARM-CHAIR, the GREAT WOOL-PACKS, the OLD FONT (7-ft. high), the LION and LION CHAMBERS, the BEEHIVES, TURTLES, SNOW-WREATHS, MARY QUEEN OF SCOTS PILLAR, and all the great STALACTITES and STALAGMITES, the gradual work of countless ages.

ADMISSION SIXPENCE.

CHILDREN HALF PRICE.

BATH-CHAIRS CAN BE TAKEN INTO THE CAVERN.

N.B.—THE CAVERN CAN BE SEEN AT ANY HOUR DURING THE DAY.

A MONKEY HOUSE

affords much amusement to the visitors by the grotesque and active movements of its inhabitants who never seem at rest, but always bent upon mischief.

PAGE FROM THE 1925 OFFICIAL GUIDE BOOK OF POOLE'S CAVERN

DAYS OUT

Excavation over the years has revealed that this cavern has been in use as a place of shelter throughout history. The name Poole is believed by some to belong to an outlaw who deposited his ill-gotten gains there during the reign of Henry VI. Further excavations between 1981 and 1984 revealed many items of Roman jewellery, coins and pottery. Brooches and other jewellery made from bronze, lead and possibly iron were discovered with objects associated with metal working such as molten blobs of bronze and hammered ingots, indicating that the cave was used during Roman times as a place of jewellery manufacture.

In the grounds of the cave was Redfern's museum (named after the proprietor). It contained many strange exhibits of questionable relevance, and included a two-headed calf from Chelmorton, the jaws of a very large Bengal tiger, the smallest dog in the world and an Indian chief's bows and arrows.

DAYS OUT

Left: THE CAT & FIDDLE 1914 67583

This remote pub remains popular today, particularly among motor cyclists who congregate there at weekends. Although it has been extended in recent years the house is still surrounded by miles of inhospitable moorland and has something of the air of Du Maurier's 'Jamaica Inn' about it.

Below Left: ASHWOOD DALE C1870 5213

Below Centre: LOVER'S LEAP C1870 5212

The proximity of the entrance to this chasm to the busy A6 road has reduced its attraction somewhat and today it is rarely visited. The towering limestone cliffs to the left of the A6 and the winding river Wye still make the journey from Buxton to Bakewell a pleasant experience, but the huge increase of traffic on this major road in recent years has made it difficult for this area to be safely walked.

Below: RAILWAY BRIDGE ON RIVER WYE C1870 5215

A view of Topley Pike with a very new looking railway bridge spanning the road and River Wye. The railway was extended to Buxton in 1863. The solitary horse and carriage on the road is a far cry from today's traffic conditions.

DAYS OUT

A popular tourist attraction five miles outside the town was the Cat & Fiddle, the highest public house in England, standing at a height of 1481 feet above sea level (500m). The pub is often shrouded in mist, but on a clear day the views are magnificent, and if conditions are favourable the river Mersey can be seen, some 40 miles to the west. Wealthy health seekers to the town in the middle of the 19th century often hired bath chairs to be transported around the town and it was not unusual to see the poor bathchairman haul his invalid customer from Buxton to the Cat & Fiddle and back again.

Leaving the town to the east, along Ashwood Dale for about half a mile is Lover's Leap, a narrow chasm through the limestone crags on the right side of the present A6 road. This was a very popular attraction during the 19th and early 20th centuries and visitors used to walk up through the small river which runs along its length.

Further east along this road is the rocky outcrop of Topley Pike. As the road curves around to the left there begins a riverside walk alongside the Wye as far as Millers Dale. Opposite the start of this walk and leading off right behind this outcrop was the Topley Pike limestone quarry. The quarry was opened in 1907 and provided high quality limestone for the building industry.

COWLOW BRIDGE AND TOPLEY PIKE C1876 8840

The stone Cowlow Bridge can be seen in the centre of this view, crossing a wide part of the River Wye. Topley Pike can be seen on the left.

Names of Subscribers

The following people have kindly supported this book by purchasing limited edition copies prior to publication.

To Ali, on your 21st, love Mum and Billy
Mr & Mrs L G Allen, Buxton
Elizabeth Arkle
David Colin Ashmore
Margaret Astill
David P Bicket
Mr Simon Richard Blackley, Buxton
In memory of Freda Boundy of Buxton
Sam & Neil Bowers and family, Buxton
Bill & Judith Brookes, Buxton
Alan & Gill Brookes, Perth, West Australia
Mr & Mrs S R Burton and family, Harpur Hill
To Barbara and Stan Byatte, from Jackie
Christine, love from Mum, 2006
Evelyn Clarke and Norman Forsythe
John & Margaret Clayton, Street, Somerset
The Cockers at Bailey Flatt Barn, Buxton
Mick & Penny Cook, Buxtonians till 2005
To Dad, from Joanne, Steve and Jack
David and Robbie, Buxton
In memory of John Dent 1915 - 2001
Carmine & Karina D'Errico, Buxton
Sharon Drabble and Corrie, Buxton
Grandad, Grandma, love Annabelle Fletcher
To Annabelle Fletcher, love Mummy & Daddy
In memory of Donald Fletcher
Len & Janet Frith, Buxton, Derbyshire
Chris Fynn
Trevor George Gilman
Brian John Grindley, 2006
Mum - Shirley Goodwin, on your birthday
Harold, Margaret and Paul Harrop, Buxton
Billy and Sandra Hesp, Griff House, Buxton
Michael Hilton JP, the perfect man
The Hobson Family, Buxton
Mr Ian Hurst, Buxton, Derbyshire
Heike Huschauer, Detlef Beck, New Buxtonians
Beth Jackson, Buxton
To the Keeling Family of Glutton Bridge,
   from Dad
To Tracy, Jane, Joanne and Abbie Kidd
Susan Lees and her son Richard, Somerset
Paul Lomas, Happy 35th Birthday, love Clare

To Lorraine on our forty-third anniversary,
   with love from Tommy
Mr & Mrs K Lupton, Harpur Hill, Buxton
Mark, love from Mum, 2006
For Marlene, my late wife, Tony Briggs
Happy Birthday Betty Milner, Buxton
Mrs Yvonne Mitchell, Buxton
Mum & Stuart Morton, to Karen,
   Melbourne, Australia
Helen & Lee Mosley, Buxton
To Mum, with love from Kay and Paul
Billy Norman, Buxton 1986-2006
Mr & Mrs M O'Dwyer, Buxton
Joan Mary Pass née Barker, for Ted Barker
Geof & Glenda Pegg, Kilsyth, Victoria, Australia
Frank & Sylvia Pegg, Croydon, Victoria, Australia
To Phil on your birthday, love Margaret
In memory of my wife, Mary Jane Phillips,
   from Herbert Phillips
To John Phillips, on his birthday, from Nick, Gill,
   Sam and Nathan
Dorothy Phillips
Eric Plant
To Betty Prince, love from Margaret
Margaret Ann Prince, Buxton
Michael Regan
Kevin Keenan
The Riley Family, Buxton
A and A Rothwell, Buxton residents
Eileen Shaw, frequent visitor to Buxton
Margery Ann Sherwood
Mr & Mrs John E Shirt, Buxton
Mr Michael Sidebotham
W L Starkey, Buxton, Derbyshire
Frederick & Sheila Stott, Buxton
To my son Stephen Sykes, from mother
In memory of Jim Turner, Trish & Stuart Bothamley
Jane Webster, Buxton
Audrey and Bob Weston, Buxton
Arthur Whitaker, for Grandad Edwin Barker
Mr & Mrs T Woodhouse, Chesterfield
The Woodroffe Family, Buxton
John & Jenny Woods, Higher Buxton PO

INDEX

FRITH PRODUCTS & SERVICES

Francis Frith would doubtless be pleased to know that the pioneering publishing venture he started in 1860 still continues today. Over a hundred and forty years later, The Francis Frith Collection continues in the same innovative tradition and is now one of the foremost publishers of vintage photographs in the world. Some of the current activities include:

Interior Decoration

Today Frith's photographs can be seen framed and as giant wall murals in thousands of pubs, restaurants, hotels, banks, retail stores and other public buildings throughout the country. In every case they enhance the unique local atmosphere of the places they depict and provide reminders of gentler days in an increasingly busy and frenetic world.

Product Promotions

Frith products are used by many major companies to promote the sales of their own products or to reinforce their own history and heritage. Frith promotions have been used by Hovis bread, Courage beers, Scots Porage Oats, Colman's mustard, Cadbury's foods, Mellow Birds coffee, Dunhill pipe tobacco, Guinness, and Bulmer's Cider.

Genealogy and Family History

As the interest in family history and roots grows world-wide, more and more people are turning to Frith's photographs of Great Britain for images of the towns, villages and streets where their ancestors lived; and, of course, photographs of the churches and chapels where their ancestors were christened, married and buried are an essential part of every genealogy tree and family album.

Frith Products

All Frith photographs are available Framed or just as Mounted Prints and Posters (size 23 x 16 inches). These may be ordered from the address below. From time to time other products - Address Books, Calendars, Table Mats, etc - are available.

The Internet

Already ninety thousand Frith photographs can be viewed and purchased on the internet through the Frith websites and a myriad of partner sites.

For more detailed information on Frith companies and products, look at this site:

www.francisfrith.com

See the complete list of Frith Books at:

www.francisfrith.com

This web site is regularly updated with the latest list of publications from The Francis Frith Collection. If you wish to buy books relating to another part of the country that your local bookshop does not stock, you may purchase on-line.

For further information, trade, or author enquiries please contact us at the address below:
The Francis Frith Collection, Frith's Barn, Teffont, Salisbury, Wiltshire, England SP3 5QP.
Tel: +44 (0)1722 716 376 Fax: +44 (0)1722 716 881 Email: sales@francisfrith.co.uk

See Frith books on the internet at www.francisfrith.com

FREE PRINT OF YOUR CHOICE

Mounted Print
Overall size 14 x 11 inches (355 x 280mm)

Choose any Frith photograph in this book.
Simply complete the Voucher opposite and
return it with your remittance for £2.25 (to cover
postage and handling) and we will print the
photograph of your choice in SEPIA (size 11 x 8
inches) and supply it in a cream mount with a
burgundy rule line (overall size 14 x 11 inches).
**Please note: photographs with a reference
number starting with a "Z" are not Frith
photographs and cannot be supplied under
this offer.**
Offer valid for delivery to one UK address only.

PLUS: **Order additional Mounted Prints
at HALF PRICE - £7.49 each** (normally £14.99)
If you would like to order more Frith prints from
this book, possibly as gifts for friends and family,
you can buy them at half price (with no
additional postage and handling costs).

PLUS: **Have your Mounted Prints framed**
For an extra £14.95 per print you can have your
mounted print(s) framed in an elegant pol-
ished wood and gilt moulding, overall size 16 x
13 inches (no additional postage and handling
required).

IMPORTANT!

**These special prices are only available if you use
this form to order. You must use the ORIGINAL
VOUCHER on this page (no copies permitted). We
can only despatch to one UK address. This offer
cannot be combined with any other offer.**

Send completed Voucher form to:
**The Francis Frith Collection, Frith's Barn,
Teffont, Salisbury, Wiltshire SP3 5QP**

CHOOSE A PHOTOGRAPH FROM THIS BOOK

Voucher for **FREE** *and Reduced Price Frith Prints*

*Please do not photocopy this voucher. Only the original is valid,
so please fill it in, cut it out and return it to us with your order.*

Picture ref no	Page no	Qty	Mounted @ £7.49	Framed + £14.95	Total Cost £
		1	Free of charge*	£	£
			£7.49	£	£
			£7.49	£	£
			£7.49	£	£
			£7.49	£	£
			£7.49	£	£

Please allow 28 days for delivery. Offer available to one UK address only

* Post & handling	£2.25
Total Order Cost	£

Title of this book . . . .

I enclose a cheque/postal order for £ . . . .
made payable to 'The Francis Frith Collection'

OR please debit my Mastercard / Visa / Maestro card,
details below

Card Number

Issue No (Maestro only)   Valid from (Maestro)

Expires   Signature

Name Mr/Mrs/Ms . . . .
Address . . . .
. . . .
. . . .
. . . . Postcode . . . .
Daytime Tel No . . . .
Email . . . .

ISBN 1-84589-119-8   Valid to 31/12/08

Free Print – see overleaf

Can you help us with information about any of the Frith photographs in this book?

We are gradually compiling an historical record for each of the photographs in the Frith archive. It is always fascinating to find out the names of the people shown in the pictures, as well as insights into the shops, buildings and other features depicted.

If you recognize anyone in the photographs in this book, or if you have information not already included in the author's caption, do let us know. We would love to hear from you, and will try to publish it in future books or articles.

Our production team

Frith books are produced by a small dedicated team at offices in the converted Grade II listed 18th-century barn at Teffont near Salisbury, illustrated above. Most have worked with The Francis Frith Collection for many years. All have in common one quality: they have a passion for The Francis Frith Collection. The team is constantly expanding, but currently includes:

Andrew Alsop, Paul Baron, Jason Buck, John Buck, Jenny Coles, Heather Crisp, David Davies, Natalie Davis, Louis du Mont, Isobel Hall, Chris Hardwick, Julian Hight, Peter Horne, James Kinnear, Karen Kinnear, Tina Leary, Stuart Login, Sue Molloy, Sarah Roberts, Kate Rotondetto, Eliza Sackett, Terence Sackett, Sandra Sampson, Adrian Sanders, Sandra Sanger, Julia Skinner, Lewis Taylor, Will Tunnicliffe, David Turner and Ricky Williams.